Check Up Tests in English Comprehension

Betty Kerr

M
Macmillan Education

First published 1980
Reprinted 1981, 1982, 1983, 1987

Published by
MACMILLAN EDUCATION LTD
Houndmills, Basingstoke, Hampshire RG21 2XS
and London
Companies and representatives
throughout the world

Printed in Hong Kong

ISBN 0-333-28863-7

To the pupil

The purpose of these tests is to see how well you understand what you read. You should be very careful to read each passage *at least* twice before you start answering any questions. Sometimes you may have to read the passage more than twice.

Make sure that you answer every part of all the questions, as fully as you can. You will find some of them easy; but some you will have to think carefully about before writing your answer.

Remember to write your answers in full sentences, unless the question is only asking for a single word or phrase.

Test 1

You must read the passage through twice before answering the questions.

The dreaded cane

physical / Mental
spiritual

Captain Lancaster was standing up and crossing over to the tall bookcase that stood against the left-hand wall of the classroom. He reached up to the topmost shelf of the bookcase and brought down *the dreaded cane*. It was white, this cane, as white as bone, and very long and very thin, with one end bent over into a handle, like a walking-stick.

"You first," he said, pointing at me with the cane. "Hold out your left hand."

It was almost impossible to believe that this man was about to injure me physically and *in cold blood*. As I lifted my left hand palm upwards and held it there, I looked at the palm itself and the pink skin and the *fortune-teller's lines* running over it, and I still could not bring myself to imagine that anything was going to happen to it.

The long white cane went up high in the air and came down on my hand with a crack like a rifle going off. I heard the crack first and about two seconds later I felt the pain. Never had I felt a pain such as that in my whole life. It was as though someone was pressing a red hot poker against my palm and holding it there. I remember grabbing my injured left hand with my right hand and ramming it between my legs and squeezing my legs together against it. I squeezed and squeezed as hard as I could as if I were trying to stop the hand from falling to pieces. I managed not to cry out loud but I couldn't keep the tears from pouring down my cheeks.

(from *Danny the Champion of the World* by Roald Dahl)

simile

1. Where was the cane kept?

2. Describe the cane as fully as you can.

3. What part of the person was caned?

4. What did he notice about his hand while he was waiting to be caned?

5. How did he feel before the caning happened?

6. Describe the caning itself.

7. What was the pain like?

8. What did the person do immediately after the caning?

9. Explain these phrases which are in italics in the passage:
    a) the dreaded cane
    b) in cold blood
    c) fortune-teller's lines.

10. The writing is divided into three paragraphs.
    Say very briefly what each is about.

11. The handle of the cane was not a walking stick, but it was likened to one.
    What were these likened to?
    a) the crack of the cane
    b) the pain of the caning.

12. a) What does 'to injure physically' mean?
    b) Do you think the person was used to being punished in this way?
       Try to explain your answer.

13. Explain what you think the last sentence means; the word 'managed' is important and gives you the clue.

14. Why do you think his left hand was caned?

15. Do you consider it was an effective punishment?
    Give reasons for your answer.

Test 2

Read the passage twice before you start to look at the questions.

Duck-diving

The Ponds are very big, so that at one end people bathe and at the other end they fish. *Old chaps with bald heads* sit on folding stools and fish with rods and lines, and little kids squeeze through the railings and wade out into the water to fish with nets. But the water's much deeper at our end of the Ponds, and that's where we bathe. You're not allowed to bathe there unless you can swim; but I've always been able to swim. They used to say that was because fat floats - well, I don't mind. They call me Sausage.

Only, I don't dive - not from any diving board, thank you. I have to take my glasses off to go into the water, and I can't see without them, and I'm just not going to dive, even from the lowest diving-board, and that's that, and they stopped nagging about it long ago.

Then, this summer, they were all on to me to learn duck-diving. You're swimming on the surface of the water and suddenly you up-end yourself just like a duck and dive down deep into the water, and perhaps you swim about a bit underwater, and then come up again. I daresay ducks begin doing it soon after they're born. It's different for them.

So I was learning to duck-dive — to swim down to the bottom of the Ponds, and pick up a brick they'd throw in, and bring it up again. You practise that in case you have to rescue anyone from drowning — say, they'd sunk for the third time, and gone to the bottom. Of course, they'd be bigger and heavier than a brick, but I suppose you have to begin with bricks and work up gradually to people.

(from *Return to Air* by Philippa Pearce)

1. What were the Ponds used for?

2. Explain the different ways that people fished at the Ponds.

3. What was the rule about bathing?

4. Why do you think the nickname was 'Sausage'?

5. It says in the passage . . . 'and I'm just not going to dive, even from the lowest diving board' . . . Why was the speaker so determined about it?

6. Explain exactly what duck-diving is.

7. Did the person learning think it was an easy thing to learn to do? How do you know?

8. Why is it suggested that people learn to pick up a brick that is thrown into the pond?

9. It is easy to get confused about 'bathe' and 'bath'. Write each word in a sentence of its own to show the difference.

10. Explain this phrase in your own words: 'Old chaps with bald heads'.

11. The passage says: '*They* used to say that was because fat floats . . .'; and '*they* stopped nagging about it long ago.' Who do you think 'they' are?

12. a) Describe what the speaker looked like.
    b) People can be brave or cowardly; selfish or unselfish; cheerful or miserable and so on. What do you think the speaker was like and what makes you think that?

13. This passage is written in a conversational way which makes the reader respond and warm to it. e.g. 'Only I don't dive – not from any diving-board thank you.' Find another example of this and write it down.

14. Do you think this piece of writing is funny, amusing, interesting, informative or what? Say what you think of it and *why*.

Test 3

This passage is taken from a story set in the mountains of Switzerland.
Read it through twice before you begin the questions.

Avalanche

And then it happened. In the middle of the night. Just below the top of the
Kühelihorn a great mass of snow broke loose with a crash like an explosion.
Slowly it began to shift, it seemed to hesitate, but only for a little. A few seconds
later the avalanche hurtled down, its path growing wider and wider, the force of
the air driven before it blasting the village even before *the thundering mass* leapt
upon the snow-covered houses and sheds like a wild beast. It lasted a far shorter
time than anyone could have believed. One moment the village was safe and
sound and fast asleep. The next, a great hole was torn in it. Part of it was still
buried so deep in snow and wrapped in such *deceptive silence* that an onlooker
would never have guessed the terrible thing that had happened. But part of it,
even beyond the path of the avalanche, had houses blown down by blast, walls
swept away, shutters and window frames ripped off and smashed. In an instant
gaping black holes had been gashed in the white village and *a white shroud of
snow* spread over its heart.

(from *Avalanche* by A. Rutgers van der Loeff)

1. When did the avalanche happen?

2. Where did it begin?

3. What do you think the Kühelihorn is?

4. How did the avalanche begin?

5. Explain how the avalanche developed.

6. What is meant by *the path* of the avalanche?

7. a) What else caused destruction as well as the snow itself?
   b) What word is used in the passage for this?

8. a) In what two different ways did the avalanche affect the village?
   b) Write out the words from the passage which tells you this in one sentence.

9. Explain in your own words these phrases which are in italics in the passage:
   a) the thundering mass
   b) deceptive silence
   c) white shroud of snow.

10. Find these words in the passage and suggest another word that could be used instead:
    a) hurtled   b) wrapped   c) gashed

11. Why were houses affected that were beyond the path of the avalanche?

12. Many different words are used to describe the movement of the snow in the passage. The first are: broke loose . . .
    Pick out as many more as you can.

13. The passage has many contrasts; e.g. 'a crash like an explosion' contrasts with 'a deceptive silence'.
    a) Find a phrase to contrast with 'slowly it began to shift.'
    b) Find two other contrasting pieces of your own.

Test 4

Read this poem through twice before answering the questions.

Hide and Seek

Call out. Call loud: "I'm ready! Come and find me!"
The sacks in the toolshed smell like the seaside.
They'll never find you in this salty dark,
But be careful that your feet aren't sticking out.
Wiser not to risk another shout.
The floor is cold. They'll probably be searching
The bushes near the swing. Whatever happens
You mustn't sneeze when they come prowling in.
And here they are, whispering at the door;
You've never heard them sound so hushed before.
Don't breathe. Don't move. Stay dumb. Hide in your blindness.
They're moving closer, someone stumbles, mutters;
Their words and laughter scuffle, and they're gone.
But don't come out just yet; they'll try the lane
And then the greenhouse and back here again.
They must be thinking that you're very clever,
Getting more puzzled as they search all over,
It seems a long time since they went away.
Your legs are stiff, the cold bites through your coat;
The dark damp smell of sand moves in your throat.
It's time to let them know that you're the winner.
Push off the sacks. Uncurl and stretch. That's better!
Out of the shed and call to them: "I've won!
Here I am! Come and own up I've caught you!"
The darkening garden watches. Nothing stirs.
The bushes hold their breath; the sun is gone.
Yes, here you are. But where are they who sought you?

(by Vernon Scannell)

1. Where is the person hiding?

2. What makes the hiding place smell like the seaside?

3. What other phrases bring the seaside to your mind?

4. Look through the poem and choose three things about which you would need to be careful in order to avoid being discovered.

5. The poem refers to 'they' and 'them' several times; e.g. 'They'll never find you . . .', 'They're moving closer now . . .' Explain who you think 'they' are.

6. In what other places does the poet think the searchers might look?

7. How do the searchers sound to him as they come near to the toolshed?

8. Find these words in the passage, and give other words that could be used instead of them.
   Hushed; dumb; stumbles; stirs.

9. The person hiding speaks twice in the poem.
   Copy out the words he actually says.

10. In the beginning the hiding seems to be fun, but it doesn't stay that way. Pick out two different lines from the poem that tell you this.

11. a) What time of day is it when the hiding game is over?
    b) What words tell you this?

12. Read the last seven lines of the poem again.
    Do you think the poem is sad?
    Can you explain why?

13. Was there a winner in this game? If it had been you in the toolshed would you feel you had won? Explain your answer.

Test 5

This passage is from the story of a boat trip on the River Thames.
Remember to read it through twice before answering the questions.

Mustard

We tackled the cold beef for lunch, and then we found that we had forgotten to
bring any mustard. I don't think I ever in my life, before or since, felt I wanted
mustard as badly as I felt I wanted it then. I don't care for mustard *as a rule,* and it
is very seldom that I take it at all, but I would have given worlds for it then.

I don't know how many worlds there may be in the universe, but anyone who
had brought me a spoonful of mustard at that precise moment could have had
them all. I grow reckless like that when I want a thing and can't get it.

Harris said he would have given worlds for mustard, too. It would have been a
good thing for anybody who had come up to that spot with a can of mustard then;
he would have been set up in worlds for the rest of his life.

But there! I dare say both Harris and I would have tried to back out of the
bargain after we had got the mustard. One makes these extravagant offers in
moments of excitement, but, of course, when one comes to think of it, one sees
how absurdly out of proportion they are with the value of the required article. I
heard a man, going up a mountain in Switzerland, once say he would give worlds
for a glass of beer, and when he came to *a little shanty* where they kept it, he
kicked up *a most fearful row* because they charged him five francs for *a bottle of
Bass.* He said it was *a scandalous imposition,* and he wrote to The Times about it.

(from *Three Men in a Boat* by Jerome K. Jerome)

1. What was for lunch?

2. What had they forgotten to bring?

3. a) Did it matter to the author that they had forgotten it?
   b) Did he normally like mustard?
   c) Why do you think he wanted it so badly this time?

4. What would he have given in exchange for mustard?

5. Was it a sensible thing to offer in exchange?

6. Who else felt the same way?

7. How did he think he would feel if someone came and gave him some?

8. Explain in your own words these phrases which are in italics in the passage:
   a) as a rule;   b) a little shanty;
   c) a most fearful row;   d) a bottle of Bass;
   e) a scandalous imposition

9. Give the opposite of:
   seldom; precise; reckless; extravagant

10. Give another word, or words, for those in italics:
    a) *tackled* the cold beef;
    b) *kicked up* a most fearful row

11. Why was the offer 'absurdly out of proportion'?

12. Another story to illustrate the meaning behind the mustard tale is given in the last paragraph:
    a) Where did it happen?
    b) What takes the place of the mustard in it?
    c) How did the man react when he was able to buy some?

13. Can you explain the whole meaning behind this piece of writing?

Test 6

Barney has discovered Stig who lives in a cave at the bottom of a chalk pit. Stig seems to have come from Stone Age times and has been desperately trying to create a fire by rubbing sticks together.
Read the passage through twice.

The lighted match

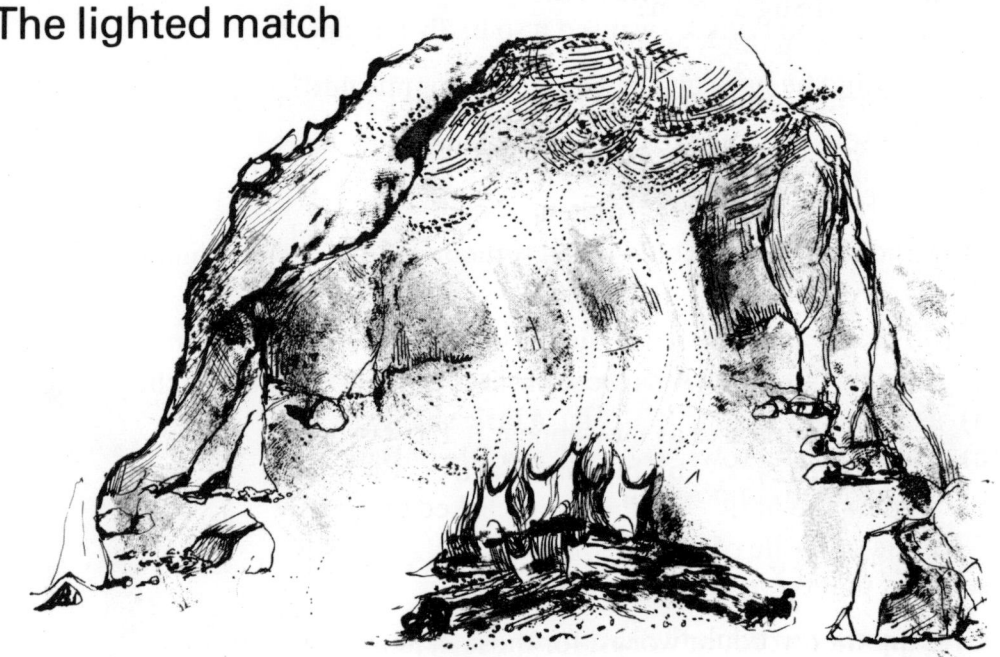

"D'you want a light, Stig?" asked Barney brightly, and he took a box of matches from his pocket and struck one. The little flame suddenly lit up the cave.

The effect on Stig was amazing. He uncurled himself and leapt to his feet in a bound, and stood staring at the lighted match *with round eyes*. When the flame burnt down to Barney's fingers and he had to blow it out, Stig gave a sort of despairing moan.

"It's all right, Stig, I've got lots more," Barney said. He struck another and Stig jumped again, but this time crept up to stare at it close to.

"Come on, let's have some paper and twigs," said Barney. By the light of a third match they found some, but they were not very dry and it took another three or four to get a little fire going. Stig was lying on his stomach *blowing like a bellows,* now gently, now fiercely, adding a twig here and a splinter from a wooden box there, building a careful pile, *feeding the fire* where it was needed. At last *the flames licked upwards,* the smoke began to clear itself through the hole in the bath and a warm glow began to light up the walls of the cave. Stig put two big logs crossed at the back of the fire, and they began hissing and sizzling happily.

Stig stretched himself out in the warmth like a cat, then held out his hand to Barney as if asking for something. Barney handed him the matchbox.

(from *Stig of the Dump* by Clive King)

14

1. Where did Barney produce the matches from?

2. How did Stig react when Barney struck a match?

3. Why did Barney have to blow it out?

4. a) What did Stig do then?
   b) Why do you think he did that?

5. When Barney struck the next match how did Stig behave?

6. What did they use to get the fire going?

7. Why did they need several matches?

8. Write down all the words in the passage that are connected with wood — in order of size, starting with the smallest.

9. Explain these phrases as they appear in the passage:
   a) with round eyes;   b) blowing like a bellows;
   c) feeding the fire;   d) the flames licked upwards

10. a) Find the two words the author uses to describe the noise made by the fire.
    b) Why do you think the author chose these particular words?
    c) Think of two more words of your own that could be used to describe the noise a fire makes.

11. Explain carefully how Stig got the fire really underway.

12. What effect did the fire have on the cave?

13. a) Once the logs were put in the fire, what did Stig do?
    b) Why do you think it mattered to him to have the matches?

Test 7

After his long journey, Bilbo, the hobbit, has at last reached the underground cave filled with treasure and guarded by its 'frightful guardian'.
You should read the passage through twice, even if you have read the book.

Smaug's den

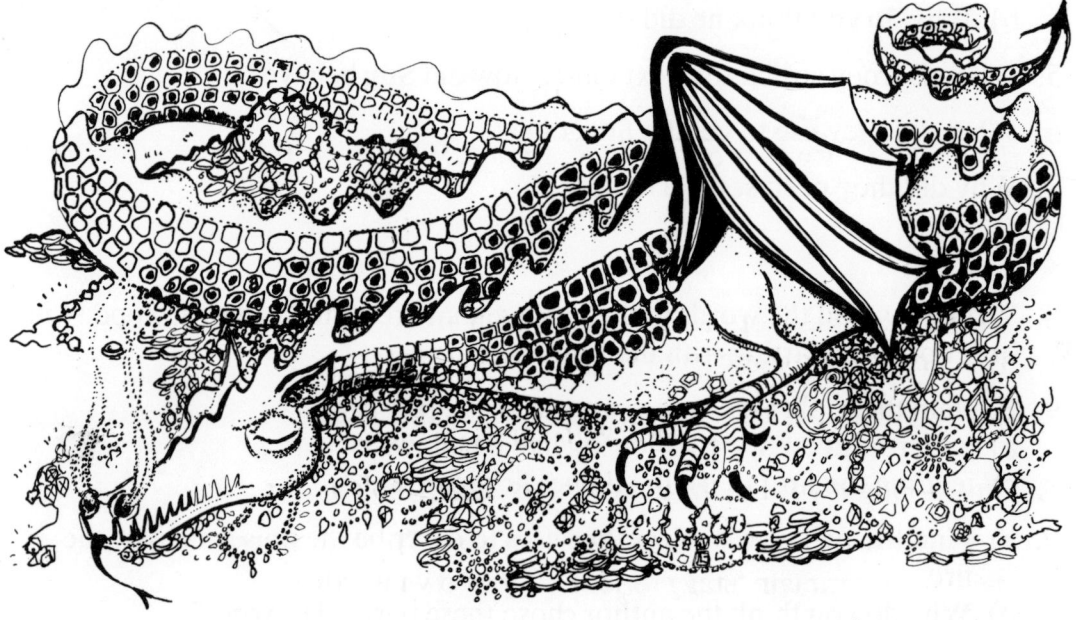

There he lay, a vast red-golden dragon, fast asleep; *a thrumming came from his jaws and nostrils,* and wisps of smoke, but his fires were low in slumber. Beneath him under all his limbs and *his huge coiled tail,* and about him on all sides stretching away across the unseen floors, lay countless piles of precious things, gold wrought and unwrought, gems and jewels, and silver red-stained in the ruddy light.

Smaug lay, with wings folded like an immeasurable bat, turned partly on one side, so that the hobbit could see his underparts and *his long pale belly crusted with gems* and fragments of gold from his long lying on his costly bed. Behind him where the walls were nearest could dimly be seen coats of mail, helms and axes, swords and spears hanging; and there in rows stood great jars and vessels filled with a wealth that could not be guessed.

To say that Bilbo's breath was taken away is no description at all. There are no words left to express his staggerment, since Men changed the language that they learned of elves in the days when all the world was wonderful. Bilbo had heard tell and sing of dragon-hoards before, but the splendour, the lust, the glory of such treasure had never yet come home to him. His heart was filled and pierced with enchantment and with the desire of dwarves; and he gazed motionless, almost forgetting the frightful guardian, at the gold beyond price and count.

(from *The Hobbit* by J. R. R. Tolkein)

1. Who lay there fast asleep?

2. a) What came from his jaws and nostrils?
   b) What do we usually think dragons breathe out?
   c) What does it mean: 'his fires were low in slumber'?

3. Why were the floors unseen?

4. Who was Smaug?

5. What was the dragon's 'costly bed'?

6. The treasure was not only gold and gems. What other things were included in the hoard?

7. Give the meaning of these phrases which are in italics in the passage:
   a) a thrumming came from his jaws and nostrils.
   b) his huge coiled tail.
   c) his long pale belly crusted with gems.

8. Find another word in the passage that means 'splendour'.

9. Find the word 'staggerment' in the passage. Think of what 'to stagger' means, and explain 'staggerment' in your own words.

10. a) What must have been the effect of colour and light in the cave?
    b) Write out the part of the passage that makes you realise what it was like.

11. What effect did the sight of the dragon-hoard have on Bilbo?
    You will need to read the last paragraph again and think carefully before you write.

12. a) Listen to the sound of these three phrases as you read them in your mind:
       i) piles of precious things;
       ii) silver red-stained in the ruddy light;
       iii) on all sides stretching away across the unseen floors.
       Can you comment on why they sound so effective? – it has something to do with the use of certain letters.
    b) Try to pick out another example from the passage.

13. Choose and copy out the phrase, or sentence, whose sound most appeals to you.

17

Test 8

In this poem the poet writes about the sea as if it were a dog; he can see that the behaviour of a dog is very like the behaviour of the sea in its different moods. Read it through twice before answering the questions.

The Sea

The sea is a hungry dog,
Giant and grey.
He rolls on the beach all day.
With his clashing teeth and shaggy jaws
Hour upon hour he gnaws
The rumbling, tumbling stones,
And 'Bones, bones, bones, bones!'
The giant sea-dog moans,
Licking his greasy paws.

And when the night wind roars
And the moon rocks in the stormy cloud,
He bounds to his feet and snuffs and sniffs,
Shaking his wet sides over the cliffs,
And howls and hollows long and loud.

But on quiet days in May or June,
When even the grasses on the dune
Play no more their reedy tune,
With his head between his paws
He lies on the sandy shores,
So quiet, so quiet, he scarcely snores.

(by James Reeve)

1. What animal is like the sea in this poem?

2. Why do you think the poet chose the words giant and grey to describe the dog?

3. 'He rolls on the beach all day'.
   To what part of the sea do you think this refers?

4. Think carefully of the way the sea behaves when it comes up onto the beach, the way it lifts and curls before crashing down.
   a) Write the two lines which describe the continual movement of the waves on the pebbles of the beach.
   b) i) Where are teeth normally found?
       ii) What do teeth normally do?
       iii) What are 'the teeth' in the poem?
       iv) Where are they?
       v) Explain the meaning of:
          'With his clashing teeth and shaggy jaws
          Hour upon hour he gnaws
          The rumbling, tumbling stones,'

5. a) Write out the line which refers to the spray coming up onto the land.
   b) What do you think 'and snuffs and sniffs' describes?

6. a) Where are the grasses in the last verse?
   b) Why are they silent?
   c) What is the sea like now?
   d) Why is 'His head between his paws'?

7. Some of the words in the poem have been chosen specially to help bring the sound of the sea to our minds.
   Make a list of them. There are at least ten.

8. Go through and write down all the words or phrases which are connected with a dog's body.

9. Why are there three verses in the poem?

10. Why do you think the writer describes the sea in this way?

Test 9

Read the passage through twice before answering the questions.

Carol singing

And I remember that we went singing carols once, when there wasn't the shaving of a moon to light the flying streets. At the end of a long road was a drive that led to a large house, and we stumbled up the darkness of the drive that night, each one of us afraid, each one holding a stone in his hand in case, and all of us too brave to say a word. The wind through the trees made noises as of old and unpleasant and maybe webfooted men wheezing in caves. We reached the black bulk of the house.

"What shall we give them? Hark the Herald?"

"No," Jack said, "Good King Wenceslas. I'll count three."

One, two, three, and we began to sing, our voices high and seemingly distant in the snow-felted darkness round the house that was occupied by nobody we knew. We stood close together, near the dark door.

    Good King Wenceslas looked out

    On the Feast of Stephen . . .

And then a small, dry voice, like the voice of someone who has not spoken for a long time, joined our singing; a small, dry, eggshell voice from the other side of the door: a small dry voice through the keyhole. And when we stopped running we were outside our house; the front room was lovely; balloons floated under the hot-water-bottle-gulping-gas; everything was good again and shone over the town.

"Perhaps it was a ghost," Jim said.

"Perhaps it was trolls," Dan said, who was always reading.

"Let's go in and see if there's any jelly left," Jack said.

And we did that.

(from *A Child's Christmas in Wales* by Dylan Thomas)

1. Where did the carol singers walk in order to get to the house?

2. Was it day or night? – How do you know?

3. What was the weather?

4. What did they each have which gave them some courage?

5. Which carol did they decide to sing?

6. What happened shortly after they began singing?

7. What did they do then?

8. Give all the words and phrases that are used to tell us that it is dark.

9. a) What is a wood-shaving?
   b) What do you think this means: 'there wasn't a shaving of a moon'?

10. Give another word, or words, for 'wheezing'.

11. Did they know who lived in the house?

12. a) How does the author describe the voice that joined in their singing?
    b) Why do you think he repeats the same words more than once?
    c) Why do you think the person's voice was as it was?

13. What suggestions did the boys make to themselves to explain what happened?

14. Why do you think they thought 'the front room was lovely' on their return?

15. Some of the writing is particularly vivid: e.g.
    'We reached the black bulk of the house.' Pick out two more pieces which you would choose as especially good to read.

Test 10

Captain Orlov has come with his men to hunt otter for their skins. 'My father', the man in conversation, with him is the Chief of the people who inhabit the Island of the Blue Dolphin.
Read the passage twice.

The agreement

"You remember another hunt," Captain Orlov said when my father was silent. "I have heard of it, too. It was led by Captain Mitriff who was a fool and is now dead. The trouble arose because you and your tribe did all the hunting."

"We hunted," said my father, "but the one you call a fool wished us to hunt from *one moon to the next,* never ceasing."

"This time you will need to do nothing," Captain Orlov said. "My men will hunt and we will divide the catch. One part for you, to be paid in good, and two parts for us."

"The parts must be equal," my father said.

Captain Orlov gazed off towards the sea. "We can talk of that later when my supplies are safely ashore," he replied.

"It is better to agree now," said my father.

Captain Orlov took two long steps away from my father, then turned and faced him. "One part to you is fair since the work is ours and *ours the risk.*"

My father shook his head.

The Russian grasped his beard. "Since the sea is not yours, why do I have to give you any part?"

"The sea which surrounds the Island of the Blue Dolphins belongs to us," answered my father.

He spoke softly as he did when he was angry.

"From here to the coast of Santa Barbara - twenty leagues away?"

"No, only that which touches the island and where the otter live."

Captain Orlov made a sound in his throat. Suddenly he smiled, showing his long teeth.

"The parts shall be equal," he said.

(from *The Island of the Blue Dolphin* by Scott O'Dell)

1. Who led the previous hunt?

2. What was Captain Orlov's opinion of him?

3. Why did Captain Orlov consider that the trouble arose at that time?

4. What did the Chief (my father) say was the cause of the trouble?

5. How was the hunting going to be different this time?

6. How did Captain Orlov suggest the catch should be divided?

7. a) How were the islanders to receive their share?
   b) What do you think that means?

8. What share did the Chief think was just?

9. Give three reasons why Captain Orlov considered his offer fair.

10. What was the basis of the Chief's reasoning?

11. Where do you think was the nearest land?

12. Explain what the following phrases mean:
    one moon to the next; ours the risk

13. Find these words in the passage and suggest another word that could be used instead:
    ceasing; part; gazed; grasped

14. While the discussions took place Captain Orlov betrayed his feelings by physical movements. What were they?

15. What nationality was Captain Orlov?

16. Who do you consider won the argument? Give your reasons.

Test 11

This passage is from a play, adapted from a well-known story.
Rat and Mole are visiting Badger to discuss a great friend who is in trouble.
Read the passage through twice, and remember that the name of the character
who is speaking is written on the left as he begins to speak.

Our mutual friend

BADGER (*to* RAT): Won't your friend try some of those pickles?

RAT: Try a pickle, Mole.

MOLE (*his mouth full*): Thanks. (*He helps himself*)

BADGER (*solemnly, after a silence broken only by the noise of eating*): I've been
    wanting to see you fellows, because I have heard very grave reports of our
    mutual friend, Toad.

RAT (*sadly*): Oh, Toad! (*He shakes his head.*)

MOLE (*as sympathetically as he can with a mouth full of pickles*): Tut-tut-tut.

BADGER: Is his case as hopeless as one has heard?

RAT: Going from bad to worse - that's all you can say about him isn't it, Mole?

MOLE (*nodding busily*): 'M (*Swallowing hastily*). That's all.

RAT: Another smash-up only last week, and a bad one. You see, since he's got
    this motor craze, he will insist on driving himself, and he's hopelessly
    incapable. If he'd only employ a decent, steady, well-trained animal, pay him
    good wages and leave everything to him, he'd get on all right. But no; he's
    convinced he's the greatest driver ever, and nobody can teach him anything.
    And so it goes on, Mole. And so it goes on.

BADGER (*gloomily*): And so it goes on! (*After a pause*) How many has he had?

RAT: Cars or smashes? Oh well, it's the same thing with Toad. The last one was
    the seventh.

MOLE: He's been in hospital three times, and as for the fines he's had to pay . . .

RAT: Toad's rich, we all know, but he's not a millionaire. Killed or ruined, it will
    be one or the other with Toad.

BADGER: Alas, alas! I knew his father, I knew his grandfather.
    Many's the time . . . (*A sob chokes him*). Alas, poor witless animal!

MOLE (*still busy*): You really ought to try a slice of this beef, Rat.

RAT: No, thanks, really.

MOLE: Don't know when I've tasted better.

(from *Toad of Toad Hall,* adapted from *The Wind in the Willows*
by Kenneth Grahame)

1. a) How many characters are there in this extract?
    b) Who are they?

2. Who have only met for the first time?

3. Who is the friend being discussed?

4. What is the problem that is worrying the friends?

5. What is Rat's solution to the problem?

6. What does Rat think is likely to happen to Toad?

7. What do you think is Toad's opinion of himself?

8. a) How many cars has Toad had?
    b) What has happened to them?

9. Find these phrases in the passage, and explain them in your own words:
    a) very grave reports;   b) our mutual friend
    c) hopelessly incapable

10. From this passage it is quite possible to obtain some idea of the kind of person each animal is:
    Here are some words describing them -
    grave, direct, amenable, pompous, matter-of-fact, sensible, self-indulgent, sympathetic, sentimental.
    Put them into 3 groups and show clearly to which animal they refer.

11. "He's been in hospital three times and as for the fines he's had to pay . . ."
    a) Why has Toad been in hospital three times?
    b) What are fines, and why do you think he has had to pay them?

12. Go through the passage and read everything that Mole says; read also the words that describe what he is doing.
    a) What is he doing most of the time?
    b) What do you think is of most concern to him during this conversation?

13. This play was written many years ago. Some of the words and language sound a little old-fashioned. One example is "Alas, alas!"
    a) Give another example.
    b) What would we say today instead?

Test 12

You must read the poem at least twice before answering the questions.

My parents kept me from children who were rough

My parents kept me from children who were rough
And who *threw words like stones* and who wore torn clothes.
Their thighs showed through rags. They ran in the street
And climbed cliffs and stripped by the country streams.

I feared more than tigers their *muscles like iron*
And their jerking hands and their knees tight on my arms.
I feared the salt coarse pointing of those boys
Who *copied my lisp* behind me on the road.

They were lithe, they sprang out behind hedges
Like dogs to bark at our world. They threw mud
And I looked another way, pretending to smile,
I longed to forgive them, yet they never smiled.

   (by Stephen Spender)

1. What do you think the title means?

2. What was noticeable about the appearance of these rough children?

3. What kind of things did the children do that made Stephen Spender's parents disapprove?

4. How do you know that the poet was very much afraid of them?

5. Did they touch him at all? How do you know?

6. Choose and write down three of the things which they did to annoy and tease him.

7. Give words opposite in meaning to these:
   rough; tight; coarse

8. Explain the meaning of these phrases which are in italics in the poem:
   threw words like stones; muscles like iron;
   copied my lisp; they were lithe

9. a) How did the poet react when they threw mud?
   b) Why do you think he pretended to smile?

10. What opinion do you think the "rough children" had of Stephen Spender? Say why you think as you do.

11. What do you think he thought of them? Did he want to be friends? How do you know?

12. Whose side are you on? Why?

Test 13

Gerald Durrell has made expeditions to many parts of the world in order to collect live specimens of animals.
This passage is from one of his books describing his experiences.
Read the passage through twice before answering the questions.

The pipa toad

One of the strangest inhabitants of this watery world of creeks was the pipa toad. I caught some of these strange creatures in a small leaf-choked channel leading off one of the big main creeks. They were so very like the messy decomposed leaves that at first sight I did not recognise them as anything living. They measure about five inches long and look rather like very flat leathery brown kites with a leg at each corner.

One of the specimens I caught was a female with eggs, and I was particularly pleased with this, as it gave me a chance to watch the astonishing hatching of the baby toads. When the female lays her eggs, the male presses them into the skin on her back which has grown soft and spongy in order to receive them. So at first they look like transparent beads half buried in the brown leathery skin. Gradually the half of the egg that is above the skin hardens and forms little convex lids, so the eggs remain in the mother's back in this series of pockets and slowly change into tadpoles and then into tiny toads, each one so small that it would take six of them to cover a postage stamp. When the baby toads are ready to hatch, the edge of the eggshell sticking above the skin becomes soft, and, by wriggling and pushing, the little creatures manage to push the lids back, like trapdoors, and then by much exertion they manage to haul themselves out of their strange potholes - like nurseries in their mother's back.

(from *The New Noah* by Gerald Durrell)

1. What animal is described in the passage?

2. a) Where did Gerald Durrell catch them?
   b) Why was this a very sensible place for the toads to be living?

3. What colour are the toads?

4. a) Where are the eggs placed after they are laid?
   b) Explain how this is possible.

5. Tell in your own way how the baby toad develops from the egg.

6. a) How is the lid of the pocket formed?
   b) What other two words are used instead of 'lid' later on in the passage?

7. Carefully describe how the baby toads are able to hatch out.

8. What are the meanings of these words as found in the passage:
   decomposed; transparent; exertion

9. To help people understand, when they write, authors often liken unknown
   things to familiar things, e.g. the Pipa Toad's eggs looked 'like transparent
   beads'. Find two other places where this happens in the writing.

10. Why do you think the lids hardened into a convex shape?

11. Try to estimate roughly the number of baby toads that a female is likely to
    carry with her. There are two clues in the passage. Explain how you came to
    your answer.

12. a) Go through the passage for all the information you can find about the
    appearance of the Pipa Toad: its shape, size, colour, texture of skin and
    so on. Then in your own words describe it in as much detail as you can.
    b) Do you think the author has painted a good word picture of the animal?
    Say why you have answered as you have.

Test 14

This story is set in America.

Mary Call is 14 years old and has assumed the responsibility of bringing up her brothers and sisters single-handed. They are very poor and fighting for survival under very difficult circumstances. A heavy fall of snow has caused the roof of their house to collapse.

Read the passage through twice before answering the questions.

The grey fox

The pig had advanced into the room, was thirstily licking the snow. The rooster ruffled his wings, hopped over to stand beside the pig, filled his throat with air, and foolishly crowed. A plop of snow fell on the bare calf of my leg and I looked up and saw the grey fox of the night before or one just like him. With his tattered back humped high and bristling and his eyes glowing red, he was crouched on the edge of the roof-hole hungrily looking down. His head was motionless. Only his eyes moved, wary and mean, following the movements of the pig and the rooster.

Something spoke to me and in the same instant that it did the rooster crowed and the fox jumped. I smelled it, its wild scent as it hurtled past me and landed almost on top of the pig. The pig screamed and the rooster squawked and flew straight up into the air and I saw my hand move, take up a splintered piece of two-by-four. The pig had slipped away from the fox, was teetering towards the door and the rooster had come down and was dancing in the snow; his terrorized shrieks rent the air.

The piece of two-by-four caught the fox square across the forehead. His eyes rolled up in his head. He reeled backward in the snow. I walked over to him and kicked him hard in the gut. He quivered once and was still.

Because I had to, I sat down again. I was a little sick to my stomach but I felt good. Not even a wild fox can lick me, I thought. I just proved it.

(from *Where the Lilies Bloom* by Vera and Bill Cleaver)

1. What animals are involved in this passage?

2. What made the writer look up?

3. Where was the fox?

4. Read the description of the appearance of the fox again. What makes us realize that he was "up to no good"?

5. What did the rooster do after the fox jumped?

6. How did the writer stop the fox and what did she use to do it?

7. The writer uses many different words to describe the movement of the animals, to help us picture the incident.
Here are two:
ruffled his wings; hopped over.
Pick out six more.

8. Find the following words in the passage and write down another word or phrase that could be used without altering the meaning:
motionless; instant; scent; rent; square; reeled; gut; lick

9. What would you say happened to the fox? Say why you think that.

10. Did this episode take place inside or outside the house? Explain how you know.

11. After it was all over the writer had very mixed feelings. Can you explain how she felt?

Test 15

Instead of hearing music when this orchestra plays, the instruments bathe the world in colours.
Read through twice before looking at the questions.

Colour music

Then with both hands he made a great circular sweep in the air and watched with delight as all the musicians began to play at once.

The 'cellos made the hills glow red, and the leaves and grass were tipped with a soft pale green as the violins began their song. Only the bass fiddles rested as the entire orchestra washed the forest in colour.

Milo was overjoyed because they were all playing for him, and just the way they should.

'Won't Chroma be surprised?' he thought, signalling the musicians to stop. 'I'll wake him now.'

But, instead of stopping, they continued to play even louder than before, until each colour became more brilliant than he thought possible. Milo shielded his eyes with one hand and waved the other desperately, but the colours continued to grow brighter and brighter and brighter, until an even more curious thing began to happen.

As Milo frantically conducted, the sky changed slowly from blue to tan and then to a rich magenta red. Flurries of light-green snow began to fall, and the leaves on the trees and bushes turned a vivid orange.

All the flowers suddenly appeared black, the grey rocks became a lovely soft chartreuse, and even peacefully sleeping Tock changed from brown to a magnificent ultramarine. Nothing was the colour it should have been, and yet, the more he tried to straighten things out, the worse they became.

'I wish I hadn't started,' he thought unhappily as a pale-blue blackbird flew by. 'There doesn't seem to be any way to stop them.'

(from *The Phantom Tollbooth* by Norton Juster)

1. Who was conducting the orchestra?

2. How did he start the orchestra playing?

3. What are the three musical instruments mentioned; and what effect did each of them have?

4. Milo's mood changes throughout this passage. How would you describe his feelings at the beginning and then later on? What causes him to change?

5. a) Why did Milo shield his eyes?
   b) Why did he wave desperately?

6. Some things change from colour to colour.
   What are they and what colour changes do they have?

7. a) What does it mean 'they continued to play even louder than before'
      Could anything be heard?
   b) What really happened?
   c) Find another word which is used in the passage in connection with the orchestra and colour which doesn't have its usual meaning and explain it.

8. There are many colours in the writing, with very expressive adjectives used with them.
   Make a list of all the colours mentioned.

9. Several things are various shades of green. What are they?

10. There are three stages as the orchestra plays. The first is when they play 'just the way they should.'
    What are the other two?

11. Why do you think Milo continued to conduct frantically?

12. In your opinion what two things, with the wrong colour, seem most strange?

Test 16

You may know that we have two kidneys. If one does not work properly, our bodies can work quite well with the other. But what happens if something goes wrong with that?

Read the poem through slowly at least twice.

My busconductor

My busconductor tells me
he has only one kidney
and that may soon go on strike
through overwork.
Each busticket
takes on a different shape
and texture.
He holds a ninepenny single
as if it were a rose
and puts the shilling in his bag
as a child into a gasmeter.
His thin lips
have no quips
for fat factorygirls
and he ignores
the drunk who snores
and the old man who talks to himself
and gets off at the wrong stop.
He goes gently to the bedroom
of the bus
to collect
and watch familiar shops and pubs pass by
(perhaps for the last time?)
The same old streets look different now
more distinct
as through new glasses
And the sky
was it ever so blue?
And all the time
deepdown in the deserted bus shelter of his mind
he thinks about his journey nearly done.
One day he'll clock on and never clock off
or clock off and never clock on.
   (by Roger McGough)

1. What does the busconductor tell the writer?

2. What might happen to his kidney?

3. a) What is a ninepenny single?
   b) What does the writer compare it with?

4. a) He takes no notice of some people, who are they?
   b) Why do you think he ignores them?

5. Pick out all the phrases or groups of words in the poem which are connected in some way with the busconductor's job. The first one is busticket.

6. The poem says: 'and puts the shilling in the bag
                     as a child into a gasmeter'.
   Does the child go into the gasmeter?
   What words could you put in after 'child' to make it quite clear?

7. Give another word for each of these words taken from the poem:
   texture; quips; familiar; distinct.

8. a) Is there a bedroom on the bus? What does the word 'bedroom' mean in the poem?
   b) What is the importance of the word 'gently' in the line;
      'He goes gently to the bedroom of the bus.'?

9. A deserted bus shelter means a bus shelter without people wanting to travel. What do you think 'the deserted bus shelter of his mind' means?

10. If you think you may not have long to live, then every moment is treasured and things normally taken for granted are carefully savoured. Give two examples from the poem that illustrate this and explain them in your own words.

11. Sometimes there is more than one meaning to be found in poetry.
    Can you explain more than one meaning for 'his journey' at the end of the poem?

12. a) What do you think the poet was trying to make us feel when he wrote this poem?
    b) Do you think he succeeded? Give reasons for your answer.

Test 17

Watership Down is the story of a group of rabbits journeying in search of a new place to live. This passage tells of one incident during their travels. Read it through twice before you begin.

Attacked

They became widely separated as they struggled up the slope. Silver and Bigwig led the way, with Hazel and Buckthorn a short distance behind. The rest idled along, hopping a few yards and then pausing to nibble or to pass droppings on the warm, sunny grass. Silver was almost at the crest when suddenly, from half-way up, there came a high screaming - the sound a rabbit makes, not to call for help or to frighten an enemy, but simply out of terror. Fiver and Pipkin limping behind the others, and conspicuously undersized and tired, were being attacked by the crow. It had flown low over the ground. Then, pouncing, it had aimed a blow of its great bill at Fiver, who just managed to dodge in time. Now it was leaping and hopping among the grass tussocks, striking at the two rabbits with terrible darts of its head. Crows aim at the eyes and Pipkin, sensing this, had buried his head in a clump of rank grass and was trying to burrow farther in. It was he who was screaming.

Hazel covered the distance down the slope in a few seconds. He had no idea what he was going to do and if the crow had ignored him he would probably have been at a loss. But by dashing up he distracted its attention and it turned on him. He swerved past it, stopped and, looking back, saw Bigwig come racing in from the opposite side. The crow turned again, struck Bigwig and missed. Hazel heard its beak hit a pebble in the grass with a sound like a snail-shell when a thrush beats it on a stone. As Silver followed Bigwig, it recovered itself and faced him squarely. Silver stopped short in fear. The crow seemed to dance before him, its great, black wings flapping in a horrible commotion. It was just about to stab when Bigwig ran straight into it from behind and knocked it sideways, so that it staggered across the turf with a harsh, raucous cawing of rage. "Keep at it!" cried Bigwig. "Come in behind it! They're cowards! They only attack helpless rabbits."

But already the crow was making off, flying with slow, heavy wingbeats. They watched it clear the farther hedge and disappear into the wood beyond the river. In the silence there was a gentle, tearing sound as a grazing cow moved nearer.

(from *Watership Down* by Richard Adams)

1. a) Which rabbits led the way and were almost at the top of the slope?
   b) Who were just behind them?
   c) Who were last?

2. Which two rabbits were attacked by the crow? Why do you think that happened?

3. What kind of scream was made, and what did it say to the other rabbits?

4. How did Pipkin react to the attack and why did he behave in this way?

5. a) What did Hazel do which helped to save the rabbits?
   b) What effect did it have?

6. Describe Bigwig's movements during the incident.

7. What rabbit seemed to take no further part in the incident?

8. Who do you think was mainly responsible for saving the two rabbits? Give a reason for your answer.

9. Find the following words in the passage and explain what they mean: the crest; undersized; grass tussocks; rank grass.

10. Write down seven words from the passage ending in 'ing' which show different types of movement.
    The first one is hopping.

11. How many different rabbits did the crow actually try to attack?
    What were their names?

12. The author chooses the words he uses very carefully, for example: 'with a harsh, raucous cawing of rage.'
    These words vividly bring to mind the sounds we are intended to hear.
    Choose another phrase from the passage which particularly appeals to you and say why you have chosen it.

Test 18

Read the passage through twice before answering the questions.

The forge

It was forever dark at the forge. Light came from the grating and *made silhouettes of all the heavy gear;* the hoists, the tackle; the presses, the anvils and the skirt of the forge hood.

Coals burned dull red. Under the grating was the bench where Grandad sat. He was the whitesmith and locksmith, and blacksmith, too.

His crucible stood in a firebrick bed, full of solder. *His irons were by him,* some so big that lifting them made William's wrists ache. But he had seen Grandad take them, and heat them, and when they were hot, Grandad spat on them; and *the spit danced* and he ran his thumb along the end to test the heat.

And then he took metal and did wonderful things, turning, twisting, tapping, shaping, dabbing and making; quickly, before the metals were cold. Brew-cans, billy-cans, milk-cans, and the great churns that stood at the roadside.

He could make them all. And he could make brass fenders straight, and take the dents from tin, and put back the fragile lion-masks on coal scuttles.

(from *Tom Fobbles' Day* by Alan Garner)

1. Who worked in the forge?

2. What was he?

3. Why was it dark in the forge?

4. a) Where was Grandad's bench?
   b) Why do you think it was placed there?

5. Exactly where were the 'flat square cobbles'?

6. a) What kind of equipment did the forge contain?
   You will need to look in more than one place in the passage.
   b) Say what you think at least two of them might be used for.

7. a) Exactly what kinds of things could Grandad do?
   b) What metals did he work in?

8. Why does it say in the last paragraph 'quickly before the metal was cold'?

9. Explain these groups of words that are in italics in the passage:
   'made silhouettes of all the heavy gear'
   'His irons were by him'
   'the spit danced'

10. a) What do you think a fire brick bed was?
    b) What was it used for?

11. a) Why do you think the writer tells us of the things that Grandad can make in the order that he does, ending with 'the fragile lion-masks on coal scuttles'?
    b) Why do you think he puts in the word 'fragile' to describe the lion-masks?

12. What do you think a whitesmith is?

13. Re-read the last paragraph.
    The writer uses certain repetition of sounds in words to gain effect, e.g. turning, twisting, tapping all begin with 't'.
    a) What other sounds are repeated here? There are more than one.
    b) Do you notice anything else about this part of the passage that is repetitive. What is it?
    c) Why do you think the writer has written like this? Do you think it is effective? Give reasons for your answer.

Test 19

This is the end of a long poem. It describes a fox hunt as the hunted fox experiences it. The fox is nearly at the end of its strength.
Read the extract through at least twice.

The Fox

And here, as he ran to the huntsman's yelling,
The fox first felt that the pace was telling;
His body and lungs seemed all grown old,
His legs less certain, his heart less bold,
The hound-noise nearer, the hill-slope steeper,
The thud in the blood of his body deeper.
His pride in his speed, his joy in the race,
Were withered away, for what use was pace?
He had run his best, and the hounds ran better,
Then the going worsened, the earth was wetter.
Then his brush drooped down till it sometimes dragged,
And his fur felt sick and his chest was tagged
With taggles of mud, and his pads seemed lead,
It was well for him he'd an earth ahead.

One last short burst upon failing feet -
There life lay waiting, so sweet, so sweet,
Rest in a darkness, balm for aches.

The earth was stopped. It was barred with stakes.
  (from 'Reynard the Fox' by John Masefield.)

1. How did the fox's body and lungs first show that he was tiring?

2. What other bodily signs did he have to warn him?

3. a) How did the noise of the hounds appear?
   b) What did the hills seem to do?
   c) What did this indicate?

4. a) What 'were withered away'?
   b) Why were these things gone from him?

5. What does it mean 'the going worsened'?

6. What are:
   the fox's brush; his pads; his earth?

7. a) Look through the extract and write down 6 pairs of words that rhyme,
   b) Explain where they come in the lines of poetry.

8. Describe what the fox looked like at the end.

9. What kept him going?

10. What did his earth hold for him in his mind as he ran?

11. What does the last line mean?

12. Read the lines to yourself again: they have a rhythm or beat.
    e.g. 'And *here,* as he *ran* to the *hunts*man's *yell*ing,'
    The heavy beats are in italics.
    a) Copy out the next two lines and underline the heavy beats in them.
    b) How many heavy beats are there in each line?
    c) Does this continue through the poem?
    d) Give your own opinion of why it is written like that and what it reminds
       you of.

13. The poet has used repetition of sounds to add to the poem.
    e.g. were withered away for what use was pace?
    Find two other examples, copy them out and underline the repeated
    sounds.

14. Why do you think there are 14 lines in the first section, 3 in the second and
    only 1 at the end?

Test 20

This is part of a play about Christmas.
You must read it through at least twice- including stage directions.

The kings arrive

(Enter, majestically, fully arrayed, the three KINGS. INNKEEPER *and his* WIFE *fall on their knees.)*

INNKEEPER: This way, your Majesties,
    Everything's prepared for your ease.
    A banquet to tickle your eyes.
WIFE: We're roasting a dozen sucking pigs.
INNKEEPER: We're basting them with brandied figs.
WIFE: We've hired a little orchestra
    to help you down the vintage-jar.
INNKEEPER: Our motto is 'Guests, stuff your gullets
    Till your buttons fly like bullets' —
    Er – your Majesties – this – this
    This is the inn. Your Majesties!
    That's only a horrible old place where I keep my donkey
    and my old bull and my rubbish – your Majesties!

(The three KINGS *ignore the inn and the* INNKEEPER, *their attention is on the stable.)*

FIRST KING: We have followed the star over mountains
    Where the stones cried and the thorns were broken.
    We have followed the star over deserts
    Where the rocks split at the touch of the night of the night cold,
    We have followed the beckoning of that star
    Till it stands where it stands. We have arrived.
SECOND KING: He will be born to the coughing of animals
    Among the broken, rejected objects
    In the corner that costs not a penny
    In the darkness of the mouse and the spider

(The THIRD KING *has lifted aside the sacking front of the shed.)*
THIRD KING: He is here. The King of the Three Worlds
    Has been born and is here.
(The three KINGS *enter the shed, leaving the sacking wide, the light blazing out from the interior.)*
    (from *The Coming of the Kings* by Ted Hughes)

1. What did the innkeeper and his wife do as the Kings appeared?

2. How had the innkeeper planned to entertain the Kings?

3. How were the sucking pigs going to be cooked and flavoured?

4. What do you think is a vintage-jar?

5. Explain in your own words the Innkeeper's motto.

6. Why does the innkeeper say:
   'Er – your Majesties – this – this
   This is the inn. Your Majesties!
   That's only a horrible place . . .' etc

7. a) How did the Kings know where to travel?
   b) How did they know that they had arrived?
   c) Write the line that tells us that.

8. What different kinds of land did they travel across on their journey?

9. Give another word or phrase for these in italics:
   a) 'A banquet *to tickle your eyes.*'
   b) 'To help you *down the vintage-jar.*'
   c) 'Among *the broken, rejected objects.*'

10. a) Pick out three pairs of words that rhyme in the passage.
    b) Which characters speak in rhyme?

11. a) In what circumstances did the second King expect to find the baby?
    b) Do you think it was as he expected?
    c) How do you know?

12. Ted Hughes uses some unusual words to say what he means.
    What do you think he is saying here:
    "We have followed the star over mountains
    Where the stones cried and the thorns were broken."

13. The way in which the innkeeper and his wife speak is quite different from that of the Kings.
    a) What does it tell you about the type of people the innkeeper and his wife are?
    b) How do the speeches of the Kings help you to feel that they are Kings?

Test 21

Although some of the words in this passage are scientific and you may not have met them before, you should be able to understand what they mean.
Read it through twice before answering the questions.

Making carbon dioxide

When a charge of gunpowder or dynamite is exploded, great amounts of gas are suddenly set free. The gases rush out with a crashing noise, and the force of the explosion can cause much damage.

But where was all this gas before the charge was fired? It was locked up chemically in the solid material until it was let loose. Set off a small, harmless explosion to see how such chemical actions work.

Get a large bottle and a cork that fits it well. Put about two tablespoons of baking soda on a small, creased piece of paper. Slide the powder into the bottle. Get ready a test tube full of vinegar. Moisten the cork with water.

Now be ready to work quickly. Hold the wet cork in one hand and the test tube of vinegar in the other. Pour the vinegar into the bottle and immediately cork it, but not too tightly.

The materials in the bottle will fizz and bubble, and after a moment the cork will blow into the air with a loud pop.

Baking soda is the household name for the chemical compound SODIUM BICARBONATE. It is made up of the elements sodium, hydrogen, carbon and oxygen. When vinegar is mixed with this compound, the chemical action sets free a gas called CARBON DIOXIDE. This gas builds up inside the bottle and finally blows the cork out.

Carbon dioxide is usually a gas, as it was in your experiment, but it can be made to form solid crystals. Then it is called 'dry ice', and its temperature is over a hundred degrees below zero!

(from *Fun with Chemistry* by Mae and Ian Freeman)

First look at the instructions for the experiment which are printed in heavier type.

1. What things do you need in order to carry out this experiment? There are eight altogether.

2. Where do you put the baking soda?

3. What do you pour into the bottle next?

4. What do you do with the cork?

5. What can you see happening inside the bottle?

6. What eventually happens to the cork?

7. What do you think makes the cork blow out of the bottle?

Now look at the rest of the piece.

8. When gunpowder and dynamite are exploded what actually causes the damage and makes the noise?

9. What is the chemical name for baking soda?

10. A compound is a mixture or combination of several elements. Which ones are combined to form baking soda?

11. What is the name of the gas which blows out the cork?

12. Explain, in your own words, where the gas comes from.

13. Carbon Dioxide is usually a gas. What other form can it take?

14. Rewrite these sentences, filling in the missing words:
    Substances can be solid like _____
    They can be _____ like vinegar
    They can be a gas like _____

15. What part of the experiment is equivalent to the explosion when gun powder or dynamite are exploded?

16. Explain the following in your own words:
    chemical action; compound; element.

Test 22

Bill and his friends are being chased through a wood by the leather-men, strange man-like beings who are summoned by the forces of evil that are trying to destroy the children. Read the passage through twice before you begin answering the questions.

The leather-men

Clear and as fragile as glass, the idea sprang into Bill's mind. They had to stop or lose everything. Suddenly, without a word, he pressed both feet into the pine needles and stood still. The voices barked at him, slashing like whips. He could not stand still, yet he had told himself he would not fall back. He ran into the din.

The sounds stung. He half-closed his eyes and made for the space between the men. The noise was terrible. Only a noise, only a noise, only a noise. He threw himself into it. He lashed with his stick as though to beat it down, but it thickened. It dragged at his mind and slowed it with fear. He ran on until he heard from his own mouth a sound like a whimper. Ahead of him, as still as a tree, stood one of the men, twenty paces away. Bill swerved. The man came with him. Bill turned towards him, took one more pace, faltered and stopped.

The man thrust his head towards him, snarling. For the first time Bill saw him clearly. Chrysalis. Not a man, a chrysalis. Brown and wrinkled, a thin shape of a man covered entirely in leathery skin. Even his head. But the skin had shrunk to the skull and was smooth, so smooth that the head was faceless without eye sockets or mouth. Yet the head saw him and it snarled.

(from *Giant under the Snow* by John Gordon)

1. Why did Bill think they would have to stop running?

2. Who was chasing them?

3. The leather-men were shouting after them. What were their voices like?

4. Why did Bill 'press both feet into the pine needles'?

5. a) What did he find he could not do?
   b) What did he decide to do then?
   c) Why do you think he did that?

6. What effect did the noise have on him?

7. How did he try to overcome it?

8. What do you think the noise was meant to do?

9. Make a list of the words used to describe the noise and its effect. Add two more words of your own that could be included.

10. Say briefly what a) the second b) the third paragraphs are about.

11. Describe one of the leather-men in your own words.

12. a) What does 'chrysalis' refer to in this passage?
    b) What is a chrysalis normally?
    c) Why does the author use this word to help his description?

13. Why is the last line so strange?

14. Why do you think Bill repeats 'only a noise, only a noise' again and again in his mind?

15. a) Authors use certain ways of writing to make their work more effective. One way is to vary the length of sentences, some short and some long. One example of this is in italics in the passage. Give another example.
    b) One way we can recognise a sentence normally is because it begins with a capital letter and ends with a full stop. Give two examples from the passage which do this but which are *not* sentences. Why do you think the author writes like that?

16. Do you like the way John Gordon writes? Give reasons for your answer.

Acknowledgements

The author and publishers wish to thank the following who have kindly given permission for the use of copyright material:

George Allen & Unwin Ltd for an extract from *The Hobbit* by J. R. R. Tolkein; Associated Book Publishers Ltd for an extract from *The Wind in the Willows* by Kenneth Grahame, published by Methuen Children's Books Ltd. Text copyright University Chest, Oxford; Curtis Brown Ltd on behalf of Gerald Durrell for an extract from *The New Noah* published by William Collins Ltd; Jonathan Cape Ltd for an extract from *Danny The Champion of the World* by Roald Dahl; William Collins Sons & Co. Ltd for an extract from *The Phantom Tollbooth* by Norton Juster; Rex Collings Ltd on behalf of Richard Adams for an extract from *Watership Down* published by Penguin Books Ltd; Faber & Faber Ltd for an extract from the play *The Coming of the Kings* by Ted Hughes, and the poem 'My Parents Kept Me From Children Who Were Rough' from *Collected Poems* by Stephen Spender; Hamish Hamilton Ltd for an extract from *Where the Lilies Bloom* by Vera and Bill Cleaver; William Heinemann Ltd for the poem 'The Sea' from *A Wandering Moon* by James Reeves; David Higham Associates on behalf of Alan Garner for an extract from *Tom Fobble's Day* published by William Collins Ltd and on behalf of the Trustees for the Copyrights of the late Dylan Thomas for an extract from *A Child's Christmas in Wales* published by J. M. Dent & Sons Ltd; Hodder & Stoughton Educational Ltd for an extract from *Avalanche* by A. Rutgers van der Loeff; Hope Leresche & Sayle on behalf of Roger McGough for the poem 'My Busconductor'. Copyright ' 1967 Roger McGough; Hutchinson & Co. (Publishers) Ltd for an extract from *Giant Under the Snow* by John Gordon; Kaye and Ward Ltd for an extract from *Fun with Chemistry* by Mae and Ira Freeman; Penguin Books Ltd for an extract from *Island of the Blue Dolphin* by Scott O'Dell. Published by Puffin Books, 1966. Copyright ' Scott O'Dell 1960, and an extract from 'Return to Air' in *The Friday Miracle and Other Stories* edited by Philippa Pearce; Murray Pollinger on behalf of Clive King for an extract from *Stig of the Dump* published by Puffin Books; Vernon Scannell for his poem 'Hide and Seek'; The Society of Authors as the Literary Representatives of the Estate of John Masefield for extracts rom the poem 'Reynard the Fox' from *Collected Poems*.